W9-BME-890

Wake Up Crap Shooters

Other books by author:

Crapshooters wake up and "smell the roses"2001
Craps and Smelling the Roses 2002

Wake Up Crap Shooters

✦

And Join the Dice Revolution

Charles C. Westcott

iUniverse, Inc.
New York Lincoln Shanghai

Wake Up Crap Shooters
And Join the Dice Revolution

Copyright © 2006 by Charles C. Westcott

All rights reserved. No part of this book may be used or reproduced by any means, graphic, electronic, or mechanical, including photocopying, recording, taping or by any information storage retrieval system without the written permission of the publisher except in the case of brief quotations embodied in critical articles and reviews.

iUniverse books may be ordered through booksellers or by contacting:

iUniverse
2021 Pine Lake Road, Suite 100
Lincoln, NE 68512
www.iuniverse.com
1-800-Authors (1-800-288-4677)

ISBN-13: 978-0-595-39083-0 (pbk)
ISBN-13: 978-0-595-83472-3 (ebk)
ISBN-10: 0-595-39083-8 (pbk)
ISBN-10: 0-595-83472-8 (ebk)

Printed in the United States of America

Wake Up Crap Shooters
And Join the Dice Revolution

This book is dedicated to the thousands of crap players who want to become expert Dice Influencing members of the Craps Revolution.

Contents

List of Illustrations

Acknowledgements

*My thanks to all the Dice Influencers I have met along the way. You have played an important part in making it possible for me to write this book and extend my dice career into the twilight zone. A special thanks to the **Kooler** for his suggestions and help with the proof reading.*

Introduction

This book is not for the beginner or the faint of heart. If you have not been exposed to the basic fundamentals of craps, you should read my previous book, "Craps and Smelling the Roses", first. Then pick up this book and get ready to learn the modern way to play craps.

You are going to learn about table position and table energy. Dice setting will become second nature to you, once you learn all the basic sets. Using the proper grip and pickup will start your on-axis toss to the back wall. Proper spin control with a soft landing will amaze your fellow shooters. We will explain what spin control is all about and how to control bounce. Advance betting strategies on pressing and regressing your bets will be discussed. Put it all together and it's called Dice Influencing. The importance of record keeping and practice will be gone over in detail with a capital DI.

I have thrown in some of my experiences while shooting with some of the best crap players in the country.

For obvious reasons, no real names are used to protect the DI's from casino heat. The word "him" in some cases may be used instead of he, she, or her. I hope you get as much out of this book as I have, writing it.

Charles C. Westcott

1

The Craps Revolution

Why another craps book? Good question! I never thought I would put in the time to write another dice book with all the other outdated crap books out there. Oh, there are three or four good ones out there and any student of the game should read them all. I'll list a few of them in a later chapter.

In case you haven't heard, the dice revolution is on.

There are two schools of thought on dice setting and dice influencing across the country, There have been name calling, personality clashes and bickering going across the internet dice forums, hot and heavy, This had been going on for some time since the early pioneers of dice setting split and went in different directions.

They used to be one big happy family of shooters and believe me they all were good. Instead of Big Red (7) being the enemy, they fought among themselves. One group worked mostly out east, headquartering in Atlantic City. Another group headquartered out west, mostly in Las Vegas. I became active right when things were the hottest.

I have many friends I shoot with in both camps. Being a Midwesterner, and in between both camps, I feel like General Custer at Little Big Horn. With the barbs flying back and forth, you had to keep your head down or end up with arrows stuck in both sides of your head.

What caused the big breakup? You guessed it!

Money and greed.. Some instructors were being paid for seminars and most of them were not. Big names in the dice world were splitting for other parts. ***Sharpshooter***, who was with PARR decided to disappear. ***Dominator*** and ***FS*** created GTC. ***Heavy*** created Axis Power Craps. Dice Coach set up shop in his home.

Things are quiet right now. I understand an olive branch has been extended between ***Heavy*** and ***Dominator.***

The word on the internet is to cool it. I'm glad because I have too many friends in both camps. I've talked to ***Dominator*** on the phone, but have never seen him in action. My GTC friends tell me he is as good as they come. They say he calls his shots and walks the walk and not just talk, I have been told this by very reliable people. I still think he struck out on cable TV.

Is the war over? Not over seminar pricing. You would think the competition would bring prices down. It's not happening. There is such a demand for the knowledge in this book and on a personal one-on-one level that I don't think it will ever happen. Will the olive branch stay in effect? We will find out in July, when both groups and the best crap shooters in the country, will be in Las Vegas on the same weekend. I'm bringing a flack jacket.

2

The Changing Game

The craps scene over the past three years has changed immensely. Everyone in one way or another, fumbles around, setting the dice. Then they just fling the dice down the table in any old manner. What are they accomplishing? Nothing! They are what we call random rollers (RR) or chicken feeders (CF). Ninety-seven percent of your dice players fall into this category. But that is changing fast.

More and more serious shooters are going to dice seminars all over the country. I attended two, just last year. Meeting some of the best dice influencers in the country was an experience I won't forget. I would say craps is passing up blackjack as the public's favorite table game and is right behind Texas Hold-Em poker.

The biggest changes in the game are how the DI's are attacking the tables with their dice-setting knowledge. Will the casinos respond to this crap attack on their domain? They already have in the smaller casinos and the grind joints. The big casinos, for the most part, have looked the other way.

The DI is trained to be low-keyed, not killing the goose who laid the golden egg. They are respectfully known for their generous tipping at the table.

The dedicated DI will spend hours practicing and will be very particular where and how long he plays. He will be selective of what table he plays at and what position he steps up to. There are eight major parts to dice control. Each part is very important to your overall success. Leave one out and you will fail as a DI.

3

Table Position

How many times have you walked into a casino and found only one spot open at the dice tables? You rushed over to the spot and immediately bought in and placed a bet? Sound familiar? Been there, done that! That is a big mistake! If there is more than one table, take time to make a careful selection of where you play. Table selection is just as important as table position.

Look for table energy. Seek out a table that is upbeat. Are the players having a good time? Do they have a lot of chips in front of them? Is the table crew friendly and efficient? Are there a lot of high fives and cheering going on? That's the table to hang around and try to play at. Never be in a hurry to lose your money! Don't force yourself into a losing game, just because there was a spot open at the table. Look for that happy-go-lucky table with energy.

Stay away from the table where a few don't players have a lot of chips in front them and everybody else is short stacked. Keep your eye open for another DI. You can always use a little support.

Once you have found the table you would feel comfortable at, it's time to maneuver into your best table position. The best table positions are the ones that are the closest to the center of the table. Right and left of the stick person is the best. You want to be in position to make the shortest roll possible. Take the time to wait until you can get your favorite spot.

Here is something to remember, if the noise has been going on for awhile at a certain table, be careful. The big run could be just about over and you missed most of it.

Again the best possible positions to play from, are stick right (SR1 and 2) and stick left (SL1 and 2). It's your decision on where you feel most comfortable.

In my experience, I have had wonderful luck, playing on Saturday nights and getting my SR1 position. When I arrive at one of my favorite riverboats, I check all three tables for energy. Usually I zero in on one particular table and hang around watching the action. On several occasions one of the table crew would ask other shooters to move over so I could shoot from SR1.

Only once did a young dude hesitate to move. The stick guy told him that if he wanted to win some money tonight, let me shoot from that position. Boy, did he put me on the spot. The dude moved and I was apprehensive about my turn with the dice. It took the dice awhile to come around and that gave me time to settle in. The stick guy put the dice in front of me with the sixes up and moved back so I would have more room to throw. With the sixes up, I turned the cubes around so that the fives were facing me and launched them end over end, on axis towards the back wall. What happened next is what this book is all about. When we finish the next chapter, I will tell you what happened. **Check out Figure 1.**

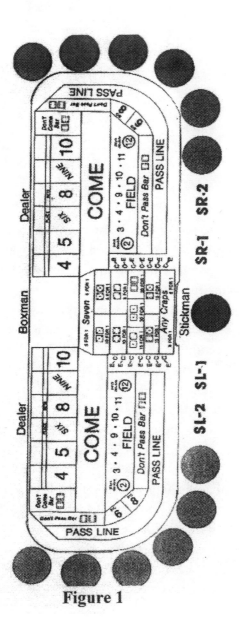

Figure 1

4

Setting the Dice

What is dice setting? Why is it causing such a concern in the casinos? To answer the first question, it's when a player sets the dice so a certain number is on top of the dice and a certain number is facing the shooter. The shooter is trying to influence the dice to end up on favorable numbers to his bets. If he makes a perfect on axis toss, he should get a favorable result.

Up until recently, there were so few good DI's around, the casino Suits hardly noticed them. Today everybody is trying to look cool and make like they know what they're doing by setting the dice in some form or manner. The more they fumble about, trying to set the dice, the easier it is for the DI to go unnoticed.

The first step in *setting*, is to know the dice. You should already know that the opposite sides of the dice add up to seven. When the stickman puts the dice in front of you for your come-out roll, watch what numbers are up on the five cubes. If you're going to set the all-seven set, then pick out two that add up to seven, Then all you have to do is turn the pair till you have a total of seven facing you.

For example: If you have picked out a four and three on top, turn the dice so you have a five and two facing you. This will give you sevens on all four sides of the pair.

Weather you are coming-out or shooting for a point, always watch the stickman moving the dice towards you so you can be planning your next set with the dice.

I have had some good experiences with the stick personnel. One night, at my favorite boat, I was into a decent hand and I noticed the stick guy was giving me the dice with the threes up. My point was eight and I was using the V-3 set. All I had to do was turn the cubes till I had a five and one facing me and I was set to go. Next thing I noticed was I didn't even have to change the dice in any way. The stick guy even had the five and one set towards me most of the time.

Another time, same boat, the stick girl was flipping the dice over and over. They take great pride in showing off their stick skill. I was having a hard time following her manipulation with the dice. So I said "boy, you're good with those dice and stick. How about giving me the dice with any hard-way number up?" Sure enough from that point on I got the dice with the hard-way up. I very seldom use the set, but it is easy to move into the 2V and the 3V from it. When she went on break, she told her replacement to give me the dice with the hard-ways up and he did.

Of course I was tipping well, but that's part of the game. A chip on the pass line when you have the dice will do the job.

Pick up a pair of dice and start practicing different sets. Don't worry about speed. Speed will come later. Some DI's can set and throw in three seconds. Most players at the table take eight or more seconds to set and throw. I spend more time focusing in on my landing area, than I do setting the dice.

Start carrying a pair of dice with you, everywhere you go. Be aware of the related number on the opposite side of the dice.

If you are caught in traffic or waiting for a train to go by, whip out those cubes and practice setting different sets. I would concentrate on just two sets to start out. Start with our come-out set and point set. The next few pages will show you the primary axis dice sets. Get to know them and their uses.

THE SIX PRIMARY DICE SETS

The Flying V-3 set – 5-2 / 6-1 Axis
The best set for inside numbers,
Good set for 6 and 8 point.
Six ways to make a 6 and 8.   Two ways to make a 7.

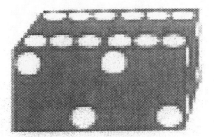

Straight 6's – 3-4 / 3-4 Axis
Good come-out set
Good for horn and C&E bets
Four ways to make a 7.

Figure 2

The Hard way set – 6-1 / 6-1 Axis
Used to make Hard way numbers.
Beginner DI's have good luck with it.
The bad news, four ways to make a 7.
A permutation of the All Sevens set.

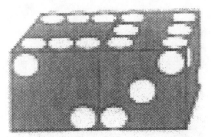

Crossed sixes set – 3-4 / 5-2 Axis
Good for all inside numbers.
You will get a lot of trash numbers.
Not a productive set. Two possible 7's.

Figure 3

All sevens set – 6-1 / 6-1 Axis
Best set for come-out seven.
Good for establishing 6 or 8 on come-out.
Forget about high/low. Four possible 7's.

Parallel Sixes set – 5-2 / 5-2 Axis
Don't Come-out.
Not good for much of anything.
Not recommended, Four possible 7's.

Figure 4

Mini V-2 Set – 6-1 / 3-4 Axis
Good set for outside numbers.
Super for picking up the four and ten.
Only two possible 7's.

009 Set – 5-2 / 6-1 Axis
My permutation of the Flying V3 set
Good for inside numbers and very few junk numbers.
Only two possible 7's.

Figure 5

DICE SETTING CONTINUED

THE HARD-WAY SET

You now have been exposed to the six primary axis dice sets and two other permutations. Each of the sets has its own pluses and minuses. Three of them are excellent seven avoidance sets and the other three sets are seven prone.

Let's talk about the **Hard-way** set first. It has like numbers all around but has the 1-6/1-6 axis, which means it also has four potential sevens for on-axis distribution. The **Hard-way** set is a permutation of the **All Sevens** set.

Hard-way set Dice— 2 3 4 5 6 7 8 9 10 11 12
On-axis Distribution—0 0 1 2 3 4 3 2 1 0 0

You can see why some players use the **Hard-way** set for the come-out and the point. You will get a good share of six and eights with the set.

When I was first exposed to dice influencing, I used the hard-way set for months and had some great rolls. Then all of a sudden every thing went south. I went back to the drawing board. Reread *Sharpshooter's* book pertaining to sets and sure enough he suggested that the set should be used by beginners. It was right there in front of me.

I compared the on-axis distribution of the Hard-way set with the 3V set. From that point on I stayed with the seven avoidance sets, 3V, 2V and X6's. The Hard-way-set should be used like a set of training wheels. Once you learn how to steer them bones, get rid of those training wheels and jump on the 3V band wagon.

The Hard-way set is great for practice. It is easy to see if you are keeping the dice on axis. If a one or six comes up, you know right away that you were off axis.

ALL SEVENS SET

Let's look at the **All Sevens** set. It has the same on-axis distribution as the hard-way set and the same 1-6/1-6 axis. We are also looking at a distribution of four sevens,

The dice total seven on all four sides and even seven on the ends. No other number can make that statement. It's a great come-out set.

The **All Sevens** set is the most powerful when in a DI's hand because he has a better chance of throwing the big red than the random roller. If you are off axis, you usually end up with a six or eight.

Another point to be noted is that your expectation of throwing 2, 3 or 12 is very low. You don't want to be on the C&E or Horn bet when a DI is setting the **All Sevens** set. You will see very few elevens. Always try to see what the person shooting is setting on the come-out. When I am with other DI's, I asked them what they are coming out with. If it's the **All Sevens** set, I bet accordingly.

FLYING V-3 SET

The **Flying V-3** is probably one of the most popular sets out there. It rides on a 1-6/2-5 axis and is noted for bringing home six and eights. The set will have the three's on top forming a V and the two and six facing you. You want to be betting the inside numbers with this set. The six and eight combined have an expectancy distribution of six compared to two for the seven.

Be careful though, because a lot of Random Rollers use this set. They see the DI's using the **V-3** and they copy them. Their delivery gives them away. Stay off them.

Flying V-3 set   Dice—2 3 4 5 6 7 8 9 10 11 12
On-Axis Distribution— 0 1 1 2 3 **2** 3 2 1 1 0

My good friend and shooting partner *"The Lazor,"* and I were having a cup of coffee in the club house, when three young fellows who work at the golf course, came over and asked us about craps. They had heard about our exploits at the casino boats and wanted to learn about setting the dice. They had just turned twenty-one and were anxious to hit the boats.

They kept after us for a couple weeks and I finally relented and told them to come over to my place for a quick lesson. I figured they would be better off with a little knowledge than just going to the boat ice cold and losing their shirt.

I showed them the Hard-way set, the toss and some betting tips. They were naturals. I told them not to bet on anybody but themselves and stick with the six and eights. They did alright for about a month and a half. Two of them stopped going due to other interests and the third had Big Red problems and was beside himself.

The next time I saw him, I told him to switch to the **V-3**. I heard he was back to the boat and doing better. If he ever decides to take craps seriously, he will be a power to be dealt with.

When the **V-3** isn't working, you have to adapt to conditions and make changes. Try the V-2

MINI V-2 SET

The **Mini V-2** is another good set with only two sevens in the expectancy distribution. It rides on a 3-4/6-1 axis and is good for sniping out fours and tens. This set will allow you to bet across the board. It is good for all point numbers. It is one of the three preferred sets for making points.

Mini V-2 set   Dice   2 3 4 5 6 7 8 9 10 11 12
On-Axis Distribution 0 1 2 2 2 **2** 2 2 2 1 0

You can see from the distribution above that there is an even distribution of two's across the board. The **Mini V-2** is one of the DI's best friends when it comes to shooting for outside numbers.

Once you know how each set works with your delivery, you will be able to switch between sets as conditions warrant.

Once upon a boat, I was struggling with the V-3 and I changed to the **V-2**. I had a point of four. I threw some box numbers and then made the four. Then I threw ten for my next point. More box numbers and the six and eights were flying all over and up jumped the ten for another point. I came out with a six for the next point. I refused to switch back to the V-3 to try and snipe out the six. I was throwing plenty of sixes with the

V-2 and wasn't about to change anything. This went on for forty-five minutes.

The point to learn here is when you get it going and you are in the zone, don't get cute and change what is working.

CROSS SIXES (X-6's)

The **Cross Sixes** is the third set that is a seven avoidance set with only two possible sevens when on-axis. It rides on the 3-4/ 5-2 axis with a horizontal six and a vertical six on top. The two and three should be facing you.

This set is good for all inside numbers but has a high instance of junk numbers. This makes for some long hands with not much profit. Check the distribution.

Cross Sixes......Dice 2 3 4 5 6 7 8 9 10 11 12
On-Axis Distribution 1 1 1 2 2 **2** 2 2   1 1 1

My experience with the X-6's has not been good. The only time I will use the X-6's is when I have the Iron Cross in play. This would bring the Field Bet into play and all those trash numbers can be capitalized on. The Iron Cross will be discussed in the betting chapter.

STRAIGHT 6's (S6's)

The **Straight 6's** has an expectation distribution of four sevens. It is great for the come-out toss. It rides the 4-3/4-3 axis and has a high incident of C&E and Horn numbers. Horn bettors love this set. The sixes set end to end like a railroad track. You can have the fives or twos facing you.

Straight 6's......Dice 2 3 4 5 6 7 8 9 10 11 12
On-Axis Distribution 1 2 1 0 2 4 2 0 1 2 1

Check the distribution on the five and nine for this set. If you see a Don't player using this set to make a point, jump all over the five and nine with a Lay bet.

I use this set about ninety-five percent of the time for my come-out tosses. You have four chances for a seven to appear and six chances for a Horn number to appear. You have to be a C&E or Horn better to appreciate this set. If you are only playing the pass line, stick to the All 7's set.

PARALLEL 6'S (P-6'S)

The **Parallel 6's** has an expectation distribution of four sevens. It rides the 5-2/5-2 axis and is used sometimes by Don't players for the come-out. I don't recommend this set for any use.

Parallel 6's......Dice 2 3 4 5 6 7 8 9 10 11 12
On-axis Distribution 1 0 2 2 1 4 1 2 2 0 1

As you can see by the distribution, it's a terrible set. Look at the lack of six and eights.

009 SET

This is one of my favorite sets. It is a permutation of the *Flying V-3* set. I call it the *009 Set* because of its tendency to hit a lot of nines.

All you have to do is set for the V-3, and rotate the left die one quarter turn towards you, so that a six is on top. What you will have is 6-3 on top, 1-4 on the bottom, 3-5 facing you and 1-4 facing towards the back wall. You will be on a 5-2, 6-1 axis. There are only two probable sevens to worry about. There's no magic about it. It's just a set that seems to match my grip and toss. You'll notice that it has the four inside numbers on each side of the dice. Very few trash numbers will show up. It may not work for you, but you can get an idea for trying some other permutation that will match your toss.

The Conclusion to the narrative at the end of Chapter 3. I left off with the dice in the air. The reason I did this, was so you could become familiar with the different dice sets. You should now be able to see what was happening between me and the stickman.

The stickman was familiar with my play and knew when I made a C&E bet, that I needed sixes on top. I felt this was a good omen. The dice landed about eight inches from the back wall, hit softly into the rubber baby bumper stumpers and bounced back four inches, coming to rest about two inches apart. It was a eleven and we were off and running. I pressed the C&E another $6.

I had thrown the dice one time and had a $30 profit and no money in jeopardy, with $12 working on the C&E and $10 on the pass line. Another good throw produced a twelve. It was another good payday on the second roll. The C&E paid $82 and I lost $10 on the pass line. I was $102 ahead and pressed the C&E $6. The third roll was a three. Collected $54 and lost $10.

The guy that moved out of my spot was smiling now and was following my bets. Toss number four resulted in a seven. The dealer collected the C&E and paid off $10 on the pass line. The stickman noted that I did not replace my C&E and passed the dice to me with the three's up. This stick guy must take notes. I set the all sevens and produced another seven on roll number five. I'm sure he would have given them to me with the seven up if it wasn't casino policy not to.

It was a roll you dream about. The come-out game produced $150 and now we were going into the point game. Toss number six came up six. You guessed it. Here comes the dice with the threes up. I believe I made two or three points and some numbers before the seven brought me back to earth.

It wasn't a long roll, maybe twenty-five minutes, but it was productive. We will go into this *game within a game* in a later chapter.

Does dice setting work? That depends on you and your willingness to practice and learn all there is to learn. When you are throwing for the point, remember this: If you don't throw a seven, you are a winner. That's right. You still have the dice and another chance to hit a productive number. That's why we set the dice to produce the least amount of sevens. Now that we understand why we set them, let's see how we should grip them.

5

The Grip

The Grip is a matter of choice depending on your physical attributes. If you have arthritic fingers like I do, there are some grips that can't be used. One school of thought is that you want to have very little skin on the die surfaces. Take the **three finger front**, thumb at the rear grip. This school teaches you to put your first three finger tips on the upper one quarter of the dice and your thumb the same way on the back of the dice.

I've tried it when my fingers were having a good day, but there wasn't much control. *The Target* uses this grip and has one of the finest dice grips in the Midwest. The problem is he takes too long settling in on the grip. *The Target* is one of the *Diceketeers* who spends more hours on the casino boats than anyone I know.

There are all sorts of variations of the three finger grip. One is to place your first three fingers all the way down the dice so that you have the dice completely covered. Do the same with the thumb. I call it the **full three finger front grip.**

The grip I am currently using is what I call **the three finger front semi-diagonal grip.** Place your three front fingers over the front of the dice with your second finger barely touching the table. The thumb only covers half of the back side of the dice.

Then press in the upper half of the dice with your thumb. Your three fingers are now just on the edge of the two dice and your thumb is pressed against the seam. To me this is a comfortable grip and gives me good spin control.

The **one and two finger front grips** are basically the same. A little thumb pressure on any of them will give you the diagonal grip.

Another interesting grip is the **Ice Tong grip** or **Pincer**. The thumb and the first or second finger are pressed against the left and right ends of the set. This set is especially good for bouncy tables. There is very little spin with this grip and less reaction from back wall. For better control, move your fingers on the ends of the dice to the upper forward corners. This will help keep the dice together. This is a favorite grip of *The Lion*.

There are times when you won't be able to get your favorite position at the table and you get stuck playing from straight out. When shooting from the end of the table, you might try the *Mad Professor's* **Long Ranger grip.**

The *Mad Professor* is one of the most knowledgeable persons involved in **Dice Influencing**, in the country. I never met the gentleman, but then nobody else has either. He is one of the mystery men in the dice world that cherishes his privacy. *MP* is a walking encyclopedia of dice knowledge. If you have a problem or question on dice, he has the answer. I will have more on him later. Right now let's look at some grips.

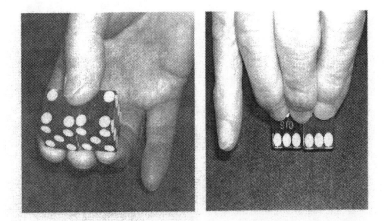

Three finger grip.

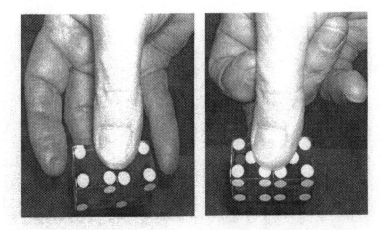

Two finger grip   **One finger grip**

Figure 6

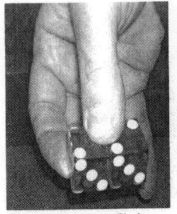
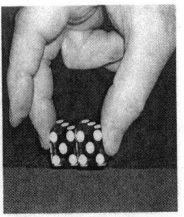

Four Finger Grip   **Pincer or Ice Tong**

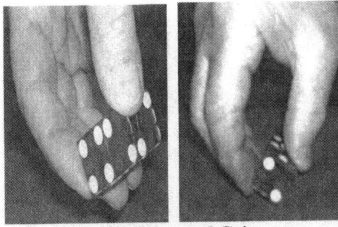

The Diagonal Grip
Figure 7

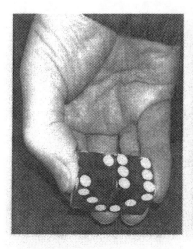
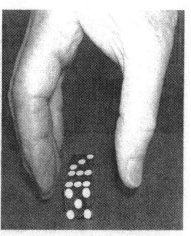

MP's Bowler Grip   **The Pickup**

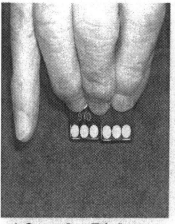
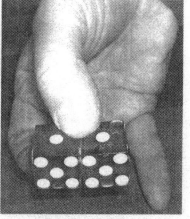

After the Pickup   **Bottom View**
Top View

Figure 8

6

The Pick Up

No, this chapter is not what you think. It's about craps and **picking up the dice.** You now know about setting the dice and griping them. There is a preferred way to pick up the dice. As soon as the stick person pushes the dice in front of you and you have them set, line them up parallel to the box person (that's the only guy sitting down with a suit on). You can also use the pass line to line up your dice for the **pick up.**

The object of this routine is to have your body in a natural position for your arm to reach straight out with the back of your fingers towards the box guy. You now have your fingers lined up and ready to place on the front of the dice, with the thumb ready to drop down on the back.

Once you have gripped the dice, turn them ninety degrees, and counter-clockwise along with your body. You are now facing the target (back wall) and ready to throw. You're in a position for a natural arm swing. This may sound petty, but you would be surprised at how many players are bent out of shape and not lined up parallel to the back wall.

If you are using the **Ice Tong or Pincer** grip, you would line up the dice perpendicular to the pass line or box person. Setting the dice, gripping them and picking them up will only take seconds. The routine should become second nature with practice. (See figure 7)

7

Delivering the Dice

Don't let the last chapter fog your brain. Do what comes naturally. Once you belly up to the table, try throwing from that position. Your arm is bent all out of shape. Your wrist is bent in and your shoulder is preventing you from having a smooth follow through.

Before you throw, you must turn your body towards the target along with the dice. You are now in a position to employ a nice pendulum swing and follow through. We are talking about shooting right handed from the stick right positions.

When shooting from the stick left positions, you can belly up to the table and your body is already in position. Your pickup is the same. All you have to do is square the dice, parallel to the back wall. You now are in position to make a nice cross body backhand swing.

When shooting from straight out (end to end), you would do the same as if you were shooting from stick right.

You also would need more back swing and follow through. The proper way to position yourself at any spot around the table should become natural and comfortable..

Try launching the dice from the deck; this will eliminate a shaky take off.

The Toss Flight
Figure 9

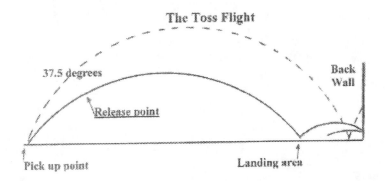

The Toss Flight

37.5 degrees

Back Wall

Release point

Pick up point

Landing area

Again there are two lines of thought on how high you should throw the dice. Most DI's will start off on a thirty to forty-five degree ascent, when they release the dice. With all the bouncy tables around, I find the lower arc more productive.

My feeling is the higher you throw the dice, the more chance there is for error. When the dice come from a high pitch, they have a tendency to bounce high or scatter. The low arc gives me more control going into the back wall. It's a lot easier to hit your target area.

The high arc is a beautiful thing to watch when it works. When it's not working, things can get ugly. It is easier to keep the dice on axis over a shorter distance than trying to keep control over the high arc.

Now you need a landing zone. You must pick out a target to throw at. I like to throw at the back pass line, about one foot left of center. If somebody's chips are in the way, ask them to move them left or right. If they are interested in making some money, they will move the chips. Hitting your target area every time will only enhance your chance of repeating numbers. The object here is consistency. We want to repeat the same set, same grip, same toss, same speed and spin. Hit the same target area and get the same kick back from the back wall. Sound hard to do? It sure is, and won't come easy.

If you have made it this far, you have your foot in the door on dice control. We are going to push ahead and fine tune this DI business.

The next thing we have to worry about is keeping the dice on a rotating axis. You have already seen how all the dice sets have a certain axis. Keeping the dice on axis is extremely important to the DI. We want to keep the dice close together and rotating equally, all the way to the landing zone. With the right speed and a soft landing, we enhance the chance of a good result.

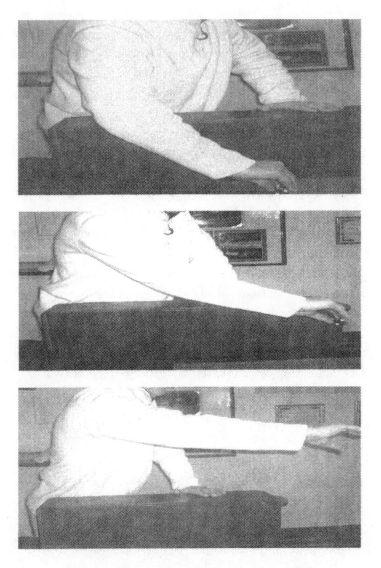

Figure 10 - The Delivery from SR

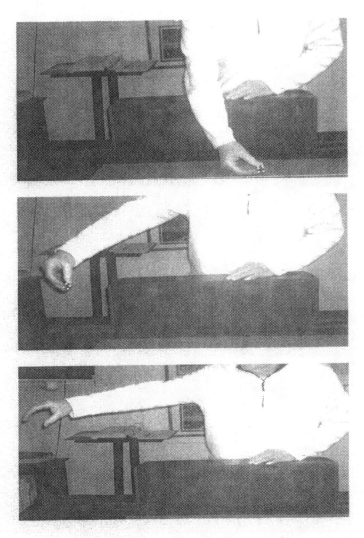

Figure 11 – The Delivery SL

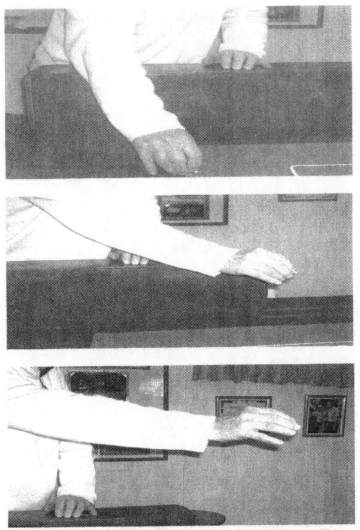

Figure 12 -- The Pincer or Ice Tong Toss

8

Spin Control

Spin control. Where did it come from? What do we do to control it? The spin comes from your finger tips when the dice depart from your hand. If you flick your wrist, you will get much more spin. This is not necessary. You get enough spin by just letting the dice roll off your finger tips no matter what front finger set you use.

By moving your thumb up or down on the back seam of the dice, you can also control the spin. The spin is necessary for keeping the dice on axis. Keeping the dice on axis is necessary to achieve what we set for.

Try keeping the back of your hand straight with your arm upon release and let the follow-through cause the back spin. Do what is best for you. Some players never get the spin right.

Once upon a time in Vegas, last year in fact, I was playing with just two other players, so the dice were quick to come around. It was at the TI and usually I am very relaxed playing there. During this session, my shooting got ugly. I couldn't get past a count of four without a seven-out. I tried everything. Different sets, different speeds and switching back and forth from SR to SL. Nothing was working. I went on tilt. From SR1, I started throwing as hard as I could. I was ready to try anything.

I put as much back spin as I could get on the cubes. The dice were coming off the back wall and stopping right in front of me.

They were both together and coming up with good numbers. I was willing to settle for anything except Big Red. I came close to breaking even for the session by violating my own rules. One of them is **Throw Low and Slow.**

Back to the spin. It seems the higher we throw the dice, the more spin we need. In my way of thinking, the higher you throw, the more room there is for error. I love watching *The Target* throw his rainbow backhand shot from stick left. It rises at least five to six feet off the table. If he misses his target, It bounces off the table. Another problem is he misses the back wall quite often.

Remember, the **dice set, grip and toss** work hand in hand. If one is missing, then you become nothing but a random roller.

The most difficult part of the toss is keeping the dice on an even axis throughout the throw. How to perfect this skill is coming up in the next few chapters.

9

Controlling the Bounce

No matter where you play, you are going to run into **Bouncy Tables**. So you better have a battle plan. The casinos are always trying out new material for their table tops. This causes the DI more headaches than he needs.

There only a few table rules the DI need worry about.

Keep the dice on the table and hit the back wall. Pick up the dice with one hand and don't swear at the Box Guy when he tells you hit the back wall.

When you run into a bouncy table, don't panic. Slow down your game. Throw low slow and soft to the back wall. Deaden your toss. Try the Ice Tong (pincer) set. Start your toss from the deck and use the layout lines for your runway. Don't hit the back wall on the fly. Roll the dice in from the start of your landing area. Give the dice just enough energy to make it to the rubber baby bumpers.

My **first encounter** with one of the "bounce per ounce" tables was at *Golfer's* favorite casino, Harrah's Joliet. We should have been aware of why there were only three players at the ten dollar table on a Saturday night. *Lazor* bought in at SL1 and was given the dice. He waited till I received my chips and

then proceeded to throw three in a row off the table. I congratu-
lated him on his hat trick.

He finally got a point and then seven-out. The random roller
next to **Lazor** showed us he could get a hat trick too. He put
three out of four off the table. He put one more off the table
before he threw a seven. The second RR got a point because he
hit another RR at the end of the table and the dice bounced off
him and stayed on the table. By now the table was getting noisy
and starting to fill up. It was so ridiculous that everybody was
joking around yelling for flack jackets and hard hats.

The floor manager decided to get into the act and offered a
band-aid to the guy that got hit by the dice. The energy at the
table was high. The RR's seemed to enjoy losing money. One
RR asked if there was a place on the table were he could bet on
the dice staying on or off the table. The box guy said no, but
they were working on it.

I finally got the dice and had a nice twenty minute run. I was
throwing the dice so slow that the cubes were attracting flies and
dust. I only had one die go off the table. The final tally for the
session was four lost dice never recovered.

Where was **Dead Cat** when we needed him for that dead-cat
bounce?

10

Keeping Records

The only way to find out if you are progressing as a **Dice Influencer**, is to keep detailed **records**. You will need a practice station or table. You also will need a chart to record your practice tosses. A pair of regulation dice is a must.

The first thing to do is determine what grip you want to use. You probably will settle in on one grip and try others, as time goes by. Once you get comfortable with a grip, pick out a dice set and start recording your tosses. Use the same grip and set for at least **36 throws.** Eventually you will want at least 750 tosses to gain a realistic view of your progress.

You can compare your thirty-six tosses against expectation figures for all the dice combinations. Here are the combinations:

Dice Result   2 3 4 5 6 7 8 9 10 11 12
Random expectation   1 2 3 4 5 6 5 4 3 2   1

What we are looking for here is the **Sevens to Roll Ratio.** **(SRR)** A look at the results above, shows that the seven should turn up six times every thirty-six rolls. It also shows that the six and eight played together, is expected to appear ten times per thirty-six rolls. This gives us an idea how we compare to the Random Roller. Here is the simple way to figure your **SRR**, You take your 36 rolls and divide it by the number of sevens you throw. A Random Roller is expected to throw 6 sevens. 36 divided by 6 is a **SRR** of 6.

So if you throw only 5 sevens in 36 rolls, your SRR would be 7.2. That mean you are throwing one less seven than most of the players out there. You are going to need a lot of rolls to establish a solid SRR. I used thirty-six rolls as an easy example to understand.

In my log book, I have 43,520 rolls recorded. I have an SRR of 8.19. This means I am expected to throw two less sevens than the random six. If you can throw just one less seven than the random expected six, you turn the casino's advantage into your advantage.

My SRR is a combination of all different grips and dice sets. I may throw thirty-six tosses from SR and then thirty-six from SL.

This is what Dice Influencing is all about. Throwing less sevens is the name of the game. If you know you average eight rolls per hand, you can plan your betting accordingly.

Figure 13 is the practice form I use for recording all my rolls. It has five columns of thirty-six for a total of 180 rolls per page.

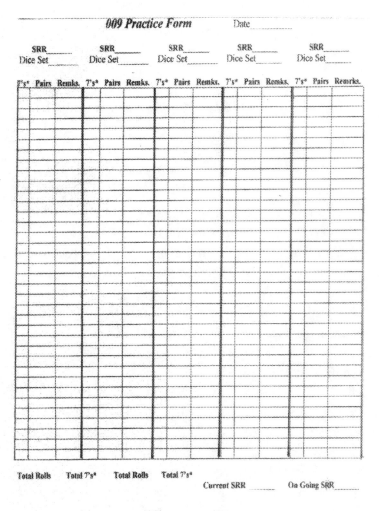

Figure 13

11

Practice Table

You need a Practice Table to accomplish what we covered in the last chapter. Practice stations can be purchased on several Web Sites. You might try Dicecoach.com, AxisPowerCraps.com, GoldenTouchCraps.com, Dicesetter.com (Irishsetter.com)

You might try building one yourself. Buy a new or used table, if you are loaded. If you build one, you can get the plans from the above web sites. As a last resort you can do what I did. I converted my pool table into a crap table…It works just fine for me. **Check out figure 14.**

The practice table will become your office. It is the place where you will develop a smooth end-over-end delivery. You will perfect your on-axis toss. Setting the dice will come second nature to you. The more time you spend developing your skill with the dice, the more confidence you will have at a live casino.. You will not become a DI over night.

Some of you reading this book, will never succeed at DI. Some people just won't take the time to learn about a new style of playing craps. There are times when I can't wait to get home and try some new grip or set. Some of you will become addicts to the game. Others will fall by the wayside and go back to their old habits of throwing.

For the few of you who try to be the best you can. be, there is a pot of gold waiting for you at the end of the rainbow. If I spent as much time practicing golf as I do craps, I would be on the golf tour. For those of you who can afford to practice a half hour a day, the monetary gain will be worth it.

Let's get back to the table. For those of you who can't afford a regulation full size fourteen foot table, you will have to improvise. If you are building your own, make sure the deck is 28 inches off the floor. Your shooting point should be 8 feet from your landing box. The back end of your box should have a rubber pyramid back that can be purchased on E-Bay or at some gambling stores. A crap layout can also be purchased on E-bay or other gambling outlets .

When you start to use the rig and you find out that the dice are jumping all over the place, learn to practice under those conditions. You will find plenty of bouncy tables out in the world. If the bounce is really bad, you can deaden it by putting a layer of felt under your layout felt.

You can gain a lot of information from the Dice web sites and forums. Try Dicecoach.com.

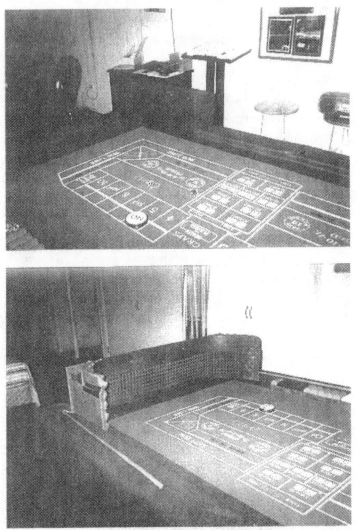

Figure 14   009 Practice Table

12

Signature Numbers

If you have started to record your tosses on your record sheet, you are ready to determine if you have a **signature number**. Just see what number you threw the most often. Count how many times you rolled that number and compare it with the expected distribution for thirty-six rolls.

...Numbers rolled........... 2 3 4 5 **6** 7 8 9 10 11 12= 36
...Expected distribution.....1 2 3 4 **5** 6 5 4 3 2 1 = 36

For example if you threw only five sevens, that would be a SRR of 7.2. Let's say you also threw seven sixes and the rest of the expected distribution was pretty much like the scale above. You were expected to throw only five sixes, but instead you threw seven. For thirty-six rolls, your **signature number** would be six.

This is only a simple example. You are going to need many more rolls to determine a strong signature number. I use a full log sheet of five columns. Each column has thirty-six rolls for a total of 180 per sheet. The more rolls you use, the stronger your signature will be. If you use five columns, you will have to

47

multiply by five to determine your expected distribution. When I started out I made up the following chart:

```
Numbers rolled.....2...3...4...5...6...7...8...9...10..11.12
Expected Random..1...2...3...4...5...6...5...4....3...2...1
Expected for 180...5..10  15  20  25  30  25  20  15  10  5
My latest 180 rolls,  *   *   *   *   *   *   *   *   *   *   *
```

* I would break down the numbers I rolled and compare them with the figures for five columns (5X36=180). Whatever number appeared more than the expected rolls for 180, was my signature number.

Signature numbers come and go as you perfect your throw. I started out with a nine and then it changed to eight. Then for awhile I went on a five binge. Now I'm back on the eight with the nine close by.

In my early DI days, I threw so many nines, I decided on 009 as my dice forum handle.

This seems like a lot of work and a lot will fail without doing it. If you are really interested in becoming a good DI, you might try using the **Bone Tracker** computer program. It's put out by *Mad dog*, which can be reached on Dicesetter.com. *Mad dog* is the founder of Bone Tracker and also one of the outstanding DI's in the country.

The Bone Tracker program is outstanding. All you have to do is enter your results of both dice from your practice records. Punch in your dice sets and the program does the rest.

You get your SRR, your on-axis percentage, your signature number, single and double pitch percentage. You can even change the set and receive the stats for the new set using the same throws. There are charts and graphs showing your total tosses compared with the Random Roller's expectant distribution.

Using the program will tell you in a hurry if you are improving or spinning your dice. The program tells me that I am on axis 42 to 72 percent of the time. Both dice were off axis less than five percent. The DI should try to keep the dice on axis 55 percent of the time.

The bar graphs show you how your signature number compares with the random roller. The program will give you an idea of how your game can change from day to day.

With a strong **signature number** you will have an advantage when placing your bets.

To record your throws, you will need two different colored dice. If you use red and green, make sure you always have the same color to the left and record that number to the left on your chart.

13

DI Money Management

How many times have you seen a random roller belly up to the table and start to throw chips all over the place? He can't wait to get all his chips in play. Ten minutes later he is buying more chips or heading for the ATM. When he came up to the table, he had no idea what the table conditions were or what numbers were hot.

Another random roller, cut from the same mold, can't wait to get his hands on the dice. When the dice finally come around to him, he piles the chips on everything including all the hardways. He's got a couple hundred bucks in play and sevens out on his third toss.

Then we have the **Chicken Feeder** who carefully sets the dice and slowly brings them up to his ear and then shakes the hell out of them and fires them down the table as hard as he can.

Next we have the blonde who fires the dice down the table before the stick guy can get his stick out of the way. She holds the dice for a half hour and throws tons of numbers.

How do you handle the likes of this type at just about every casino you play at? Here's how I would handle the four of them. The two "money bags" I would not play. I would not even give them the satisfaction of the five count. As for the other two, I would go fishing. After the come-out, I would place the eight at table minimum for two or three throws. If they hit the eight I would ride out the storm. If they hit it again, I would spread to the six and play on the casino money from that point on.

What's all this got to do with Money Management? We can learn a lot from the obvious mistakes the two "money bags" made. The chicken feeder was a gamble and the blonde slinger got lucky and paid off. Remember this. **Don't be in a hurry to lose your money.** There will always be another roll of the dice. How much you can afford to bet is the key. Never bet with scared money. If you are scared you will lose, you will lose. Above all else, don't bet on every shooter at the table.

Don't come to the table with twenty dollars and expect to win a fortune. You have to set yourself a **stop loss** number and abide by it. If your bankroll for the session is $200, your stop loss would be $100…If it was $1,000, the stop loss would be $500. The point is to have a plan and stick with it. There is no fast cut rule. If the bankroll is small, then the bets have to be small. This is not a game of all in on one roll. Never go into your pocket once you have bought in.

Money Management goes hand in hand with betting strategy, which is next up.

14

DI Betting Strategy

Betting strategy is closely related to money management. You have to manage your betting to match your bankroll for that session. You should insert a stop loss just like you would if playing the stock market. Let's look at some of the strategies I use during a session.

If I have the dice or a proven DI has the dice, I like to play a **game within a game.** The first game is the come-out roll. I put $10 on the pass line and $6 on the C&E. If I throw a craps number, a seven or eleven, I will have a payday. If a point number comes up, I lose my C&E bet. By setting the **straight six** set (rich in sevens) I have one chance in three of winning on the first roll. Should I hit on the C&E, I would press it another $6. I've had rolls where I tossed 2, 3, 7, 11, and 12, six or seven times before throwing a point number. This play is a game by itself,

The second part of the game is when you establish a point number. Now I would take odds on my pass line and place the six and eight. I like the eight because that's my current signature number. If the eight comes right back, I would press it. Once I have my initial money off the table, I would press one unit on each number as it hit. Some of my cohorts believe you should press fifty percent. I like to salt away more than I have on the table. I'm a firm believer in getting my money off the table as soon as possible. I use this style of play when I have the dice or I have confidence in some DI.

DI Regression betting is the way of life for the DI. By knowing your **SRR** and the **SRR** of your fellow DI's, you are able to bet larger sums with confidence. You have to be observant or know in advance what sets they will be using. We are looking for a realistic SRR of 7.5.over a long period of tracking rolls.

This time we will not make a pass line bet. After the point has been established, we will place $88 inside (5, 6, 8, and 9). One hit and you win $28. Now you have to make a decision. Wait for another hit or regress to $44 inside. By regressing to $44 you now have only $16 in jeopardy. It will take one more hit to break even (-$2). If you get two hits in the first four rolls, you will have the best of it. We are looking for at least seven rolls out of a DI. After the third hit, you can start pressing each number as it hits. The object is to get our money out of play ASAP.

If you are at a $5 table you can start by placing $44 inside and as soon as you get a hit or two, regress down to $22 inside. Think about this for a minute. Some players over the years would make a $5 pass line bet with double odds and make two come bets with double odds. That totals $45 and took at least three rolls to establish. We can establish four numbers on the first roll and save a dollar.

Come betters are a dying breed. They are waking up to the fact that they can win more by placing bets of equal amounts as to what they would have bet on the come.

Progression betting by a DI can be very profitable but it can also be very hazardous to the health of your bankroll. For example, you are at a $10 table and you place the six and eight for $12 each. The six hits for $14 and you press it $12. You now have $24 working on the six and $2 in the tray. If the eight hits, you press it like the six. On the second hit on the six you go to $48 and put $4 in the tray. From this point on you have many options. The next hit you can bring home the $56 or press fifty percent of it. Either way you will have your initial bet out of the game.

How far you want to take this progression is a matter of choice or fortitude. Your bailing out is also based on your SRR. Hitting three six or eights is not too uncommon. It can be very rewarding and the worst case scenario is you lose $24.

Betting **outside numbers** (4, 5, 9, and 10) should be approached by DI's who have a very strong SRR with particular dice sets. **Don't betters** love the four and ten They will lay the four and ten even on the come-out. If you see a DI setting the V-2 set when he has a four or ten for his point, consider placing either one.

The Iron Cross strategy is another favorite of mine. When I have the dice and my point is five, six or eight, I will work into setting it up. Conditions must be right for it to work out or you will be looking at a loss. If I was at a $10 table, I would take double odds on my pass line bet. If the point was six, I would place the five ($15) and place the eight ($18). Then I would make a $10 field bet. Now any number that comes up is a payday except for the seven. This ploy is especially good when a lot of junk numbers are coming up. You are collecting all the time while you're waiting for the five, six and eight to hit.

You must be careful how and when you make the play. If the five, six and eights are hitting, you have to be aware of that $10 field bet dragging down profits.

Using the **Iron Cross** can be a drain on your funds if not used properly. You have to use good judgment when laying that field bet down. I like to wait until I have at least three or four units on the place numbers before I put that field bet into play.

I've had nights where I have thrown six or seven junk numbers in a row. That $10 Field bet covered the rest of my bets on the table.

It's great when everything falls in place and you are receiving a paycheck on every throw. Meanwhile everyone else at the table is trying to figure out what you're doing.. **Figure 15** on the next page shows you what it looks like.

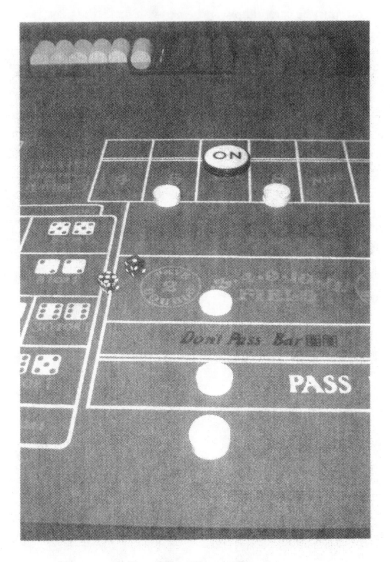

Figure 15 – The Iron Cross

15

To Bet or Not to Bet

To bet or not to bet is the question. The DI is trained not to bet every shooter. Instructors tell them to only bet on themselves. What they are saying is, "do as I say, not as I do." They also tell us to play at tables that are empty or only have a couple shooters. This is all good and well in theory. In reality don't bet on it. I'm not a person who will get up before the sun to shoot craps.

When in Vegas, I will get up and play at 7:30-8:00 a.m. after I get my Starbucks coffee. On my last visit to my favorite casino I went for what I call a early morning shoot. Sure enough there was only one table ready for play and was empty. I personally don't like to play alone. I like table energy and camaraderie.

Well, I decided to go it alone and to see what happens. While I was buying in, I asked the box suit how many practice throws I was allowed. He said as many as I want as long as I have $10 on the pass line. I put $10 on the pass line and threw a six and then seven-out. After fifteen minutes of point seven-out and $100 poorer, I moved over to SL and proceeded to lose another $100. I was so bad that the Floor Suit watching offered some advice and said to throw the dice a little higher. I was already at my stop loss and was looking for a way to disappear.

I was just about ready to pack it in, when four other shooters joined the table. I moved back to SR and watched the four shoot. Two of them had nice tosses and were setting what looked like the X-6's. I decided to stay. They made a few numbers before Big Red showed up.

When the dice came to me, I decided to give it one more chance. I don't remember changing anything, but I went on a thirty minute run. The other players were whooping it up and the table energy was running high. I had bought in for $300 and colored out a little over $500. The box guy and the Suit said that I made a good come back after the way I started out. I said, I suppose that means you won't pop for breakfast. He said no problem, be right back. You have to keep your cool and not go on tilt. Patience is a must in craps.

That particular morning session was not a ringing endorsement for me to play by myself. If you were ice cold like I was, your buy-in would disappear fast. Plus the Suits get to watch you make throw after throw. I wouldn't say that was staying under the radar. How do you feel after you seven-out? I had that sinking feeling. I'm sure it hurt my next throw. To seven-out so many times in that short period of time has to be upsetting. I need a little time to get re-focused and the RR serves that purpose.

Betting other DI's can be hazardous to your bankroll. It's a good policy to qualify them like everyone else. If one should get hot, by working your strategy, you will be on board when it happens. In the mean time, be patient and don't go on tilt.

16

Betting On RR's and CF's

The best defense **on betting random rollers and chicken feeders** is don't bet on them, Now we all know that this is the hardest thing to do. You're at a full table and no where else to play, what are you going to do? If you must play under these conditions I suggest you do one or all of the following strategies: Don't bet on every shooter. Pick and choose. Watch what the shooter did on his first roll. Did he set the dice? How was his grip and toss?

With this information you can decide whether you want to bet on him or not. If you are at a table full of RR's, skip every other one. The least amount of play on them will save you money.

I watch for a shooter who has just thrown two or three sevens. What are the chances of him throwing another seven, right away? You might be able to catch a six or eight in the next couple rolls and then come down.

When I decide to bet on a RR, I will place the eight for $12. If the eight doesn't hit in two or three tosses, come down. If the eight hits, I have three options. I could press the eight or spread to the six and put $2 in the tray or come down with a $14 profit. Whatever route I take, I will not lose more than $12 on a random-chicken-feeding roller. If I press the bet and it hits, I am $20 ahead and no money in jeopardy.

If there are fourteen players at the table and I can eliminate seven of them by not betting on them, that's money in the bank. The remaining six might be made up of two shooters with potential, two RR's and two DI's. That's a $72 loss if those six bomb out. I like my chances though it will be a long wait for the dice to come around.

What about the infamous **Five Count?** I suggested its use in my second book with modifications. That was five years ago and a whole new school of thought has surfaced since then. At the time it was new and shooters were just finding out about it. Nobody really analyzed it. If they did, they were only telling one side of it.

The one fact is that 50% of the random rollers will seven-out within the five-count. What about the other 50% of the RR's? Now that you know what the SRR is all about, it should be obvious what's wrong with it.

On the sixth roll everybody would load up on odds, put out come bets and start placing numbers. What's wrong with this picture? The RR has a SRR of six. The seven is overdue and the dedicated five counters are putting more chips out there. Doesn't it make since that if a random roller is expected to seven-out in six throws, the clock is ticking on every throw after five? That's why we work so hard to improve our SRR and acquire one, two or three more rolls than the RR.

In the teachings of the grand master of craps, the *Mad Professor*, you would learn that if you must play RR's, use a **Regression Strategy.** Pick and choose your spot by qualifying each shooter. **Use regression before progression to eliminate depression.**

Limited use of the **Five-Count** is recommended. If a hot shooter comes along, you will be jumping in a day late and a dollar short. If the table is ice cold, you would be better off jumping to the dark side and playing the **Don't Pass or Come.** If the table is choppy, your bankroll may need refinancing. Then there will be sessions where everybody is throwing eight or nine tosses before big red shows up.

Personally I don't use the Five-Count any more. When I decide to play a shooter, I'm all in from the beginning or I'm all out. That includes the potential one unit bet on the eight.

The argument goes on. To "five count or not to five count." Actually the Five-Count is more like the six, seven or eight count, if you take into consideration the non-point numbers that could be thrown before the point is established. Now we're talking about jumping into a game that possibly used up eight tosses. Check your log book. How many of your hands have gone longer than nine? Not many, I bet.

You can get two or three hits during the first eight tosses and regress down so you have a profit and no chips in jeopardy.

Craps is a random design game with the edge going to the casino. They get their edge from the payoff percentages they impose. If we can throw one less seven than expectation, we turn the odds in our favor.

17

Hit and Run Craps

How many times have you stayed at the table too long and gave all your winnings back? I know, been there, done that. Stop-losses are there for you to ease the pain when in a losing mode. It's hard to quit when you are ahead. Ask yourself, how much is enough? Better yet, when you buy in for $200, set your stop loss at $100, Lets say you are $200 ahead. You now have $400 so set your stop-loss at $300. That way you are locking up a $100 profit and have $100 to play with.

$100 isn't much to play with but you can adjust to higher figures and the stop-loss can vary. For example if my buy in was for $300 I would set the stop-loss at $100. The idea is to not get tapped out. You will feel better about yourself because you had the discipline to walk away with $100 left from that losing session.

The best **Hit and Run** player in the country is the *Irish setter*. He was the creator of Dicesetter.com, a Web Site that is recognized as having the best information on craps and dice setting.

I have rolled the bones with *Irish setter* and consider him one of the best dice players west of the Mississippi. I say that, because I'm east of the Mississippi. Just kidding, *Irish,* you are one of the best in the country. When it comes to **Hit and Run**, you are tops. If you are at the table with *Irish* and turn away for a second, he's gone. Fifteen minutes later, he's back at the other end of the table. He can disappear faster than *Heavy* putting away a beer.

Heavy's the guy you want at your table when things go wrong. He is the king of the Don't players. When you talk about seminars on dice influencing, *Heavy* is at the top of the list. While playing next to him I learned the game within the game strategy and how to play the Horn and World bets on DI's. *Heavy's* Web site, Axispowercraps.com is right up there with Irishsetter.com.

These gentlemen know when to exit a game. If you just had a big run, then its time to color up and exit. If someone else has a long roll, color up. Long rolls are few and far in between. Very seldom will you see back to back long rolls.

Just recently at the Majestic Star casino, I was approaching the crap tables when the person in my SR1 spot walks away. Then I noticed several shooters were coloring up. I asked the guy next me how things were going. He said the guy who just left my spot had a monster roll. The red flag went up and I started looking for another table. I didn't hit, but I did run.

18

Tipping

Tipping can help you or hurt you, depending on how you use your chips. If you tip with discretion, you will be respected by the crew. They might look the other way when you come up short of the back wall or too slow setting the dice. With proper tipping, the Stick might set the dice for you with certain numbers up. The dealer will remind you of bets you might of forgotten to make in your normal pattern of play.

I make solid bets for the crew that have a chance of winning. I would bet the pass line with odds or the six and eight. I would make sure that if the point was five or nine, I had two chips on the odds so they would get the extra chip. I only tip when I have the dice. If my roll is decent, I would make a two-way hard-way bet. Never would I bet a chip alone on the hard-way for the crew. Their thinking is if I am not betting it, I must not have confidence in the bet.

You want to tell the stick that you got them piggyback on the line. That way the chip stays with the line bet till you seven-out. The crew collects only the winnings but they always have something going. I very seldom tip when I leave the table. .You should tip during your play. Tipping when you leave the table won't do you any good, you're gone. If you don't tip while you are in play, you have lost your tip advantage. Tipping after you are done gains you nothing. If you are a red chip player and buy in for $2-$300, you only need to bet two chips per pass line play with odds.

Tipping well within my means and play, I receive respect from the crew. So many nights I witnessed the entire table neglecting to tip. I would be the only guy tipping. One crazy Saturday night, that was the scene. The guy next to me was betting green chips and was doing real well but never put a bet out there for the crew. The stick person was dumping the dice in front of me so the guy had to reach way over to pick them up. He finally said to the stick, would you please push the dice where I can pick them up. I saw the opening and took it. I said to the guy, if you would put a white chip out on the pass line once in a while for the crew, you might receive the dice in front of you.

The guy seemed nice enough but he had no clue about tipping. He put a white chip down on the pass line. The stick guy smiled and put the dice right in front of the guy. The Stick whispered thanks. Most of the table saw what happened and what do you know, four more white chips hit the pass line.

My GTC trained friend, the **Target**, is a generous tipper. I always enjoy playing with him. By the time I get to the table, he already has the crew eating of his hand. He usually has a chair at the table. This particular night the **Target** left early and told me to go ahead and use his chair. I used his chair about a half hour.

A week later at the same boat, we were buying in and the dealer asked if I wanted a chair tonight. I said sure. Five minutes later, here comes one of the Suits with the chair. Since then I had them put a doctor's note in their computer for a chair if needed. **Tipping** is one of your tools of the trade. We tip so the crew will give us favorable treatment. Tip only when you have the dice.

19

Table Manners

Table Manners at the crap table can be another tool that will get you favorable treatment. When the Suit hands back your players card and says good luck, acknowledge him with a thank you. Always be on alert for an opening to develop a rapport between you and the Suit and crew.

Once when I was handed back my players card I told the Suit I liked his tie. He said, I like your sweater. The closest dealer said, that's cool, where did you get it? I said, I don't know, the wife dresses me. This opened the line of communications for the entire session.

When buying in, make sure nobody is throwing the dice when you set your money down. You might wait till the shooter sevens-out before putting your buy-in on the table. That's just one less shooter you have to worry about.

Here's a tip for all you SR1 shooters. When the Stick person is serving the dice to SR2, 3, and 4(the hook), move back and give him room to work his stick. The same goes for when SR2 has the dice. Be considerate of the other shooters.

Don't wait until the last minute to place your bet. On the same line, don't push your bet out there while the dealer is still paying off. Be aware of the order the dealer pays off. Be polite when pointing out an error in payoffs. Try to be tolerant of other shooters. When someone sevens-out, suppress the urge to tell the shooter he sucks. You probably shouldn't have bet on him in the first place. On the same note, when a shooter does well, let him know it. An occasional high-five is good.

This chapter brings to mind an experience I had on a crazy Saturday night at the boat. *Lazor* was at SL1 and I was at SR1. I had just got the dice and was setting for my come-out roll. Down at the end of the table, this loud voice yells out, "Come on shooter and just throw the dice." I was just about to throw and decided to stall and regroup. At this point *Lazor* tells the guy to shut up and take notes and he might learn something. The big guy says, "I'm not talking to you." *Lazor* fires back, "well I'm talking to you."

One of the pit critters was watching from behind the box guy. He happened to be one of the Suits that up-graded my player card. I could see it coming. The Suit goes over to the guy and tells him that if he was in a hurry to be someplace, he should go now or keep quiet and play his own game.

I went on and had a nice twenty minute run. The big guy never said a word after that. I told *Lazor* to pick on smaller guys in the future.

This noisy guy lacked patience and obviously was playing with scared money and lacked **Table Manners**.

Dealing with smokers can be a problem. The best answer came from *Heavy* on his own Power Axis Craps web site. *Heavy* relates when he plays early morning sessions, he orders bottled water from the waitress and discreetly pours a little water in the nearby ash trays. I think coffee would do just as well.

20

Casino Heat

Casino Heat can arise at any time and without warning. It can come from anyone on the table crew or any of the pit creatures. It can be verbal harassment or direct orders. It might even be in the form of casual comments.

The most common heat comes from not hitting the back wall with both dice. To me, this is one of the biggest fallacies in Craps.

The pit creatures insist that the table crew enforce this rule. Why is beyond me. When only one die hits the wall, it becomes a random roll. Isn't this what the casinos want? The DI wants both dice to hit the back wall.

Setting the dice is becoming common place with almost all shooters. They set some number and then just fling them down the table. In reality they are helping the DI by their actions. With everybody fiddling with the dice, the DI becomes invisible. We try to blend in with the chicken feeders.

I was playing at the IP one night with **Phil** and **Jim** at an empty table. The place was empty, which was very strange. I got a nice little run going and was about $200 ahead when **Phil** says, "it looks like you are drawing a lot of attention." I looked up and sure enough there were three Suits intently watching

every move we made. I remarked that it looked like a suit con-
vention. This is what I call observing heat. To avoid any problems, we decided to leave. I never did like the IP's layout or how
dark it was. I hope Harrah's improves it.

When it comes time to go on a heat-seeking tour, there is no
better guide than **Hot Shooter**. I had the pleasure of playing
with him after Craps fest 2005. We played in several downtown
casinos and did not draw any heat. We were both pressed for
time and had no chance to get hot. This is a good spot to take a
break and head out to Trump's boat and see if conditions have
changed since the Majestic Star bought DT out.

We arrive around 7 pm and were surprised that there were
openings at the only table working. One of the dealers said,
"Call for a chip fill, the **Diceketeers** are in the building." **Target**
was already sitting at SL1 and **Lazor** moved in at SL2. I manage
to finally get in at SR2 while **Target** was warming up the crowd
with his high arc toss.

The table crew was friendly and knew us from previous sessions. We started off with **Target** rolling for twenty minutes.
Then **Lazor** put in a twenty minute roll. A CF was next and he
had the dice for fifteen minutes. Target yells, "Hey Charlie, you
may not get the dice for another hour." I told him, "that's okay,
but when I do get them, you might not see the dice for another
hour."

When I did get the dice, I rolled for forty-five minutes. One
hour later I had a two minute roll. My third roll was another
forty-five minutes with the Suits starting to congregate. They
watched for awhile and turned away, shaking their heads. What
I was doing was changing my grip on the dice. I used the pincer
on my come-out and the three finger diagonal on the points.

This seemed to defuse the situation and the Suit offered us three dinners. We played four and a half hours and cashed eight or nine big ones.

I would say no real heat was involved.

21

Comps and Player Cards

Complimentary rewards are for you're continuous contribution to the well being of the casinos. They are known as **Comps.** They come in the form of free night stays at the casino, airfare, meals, show tickets, line passes and all sorts of other goodies.

It all starts with the **player's card**. All DI's should have one for every casino they play in. If for no other reason, it usually will get you the casino rate for your rooms. Comps have become a way of life in the casino world.

You call for room reservations and the first thing they ask you, do you have a players card? When you buy in at the crap tables, the first thing they ask you is, do you have a card? If you don't, they ask you if you want one. If you want to play slots or poker machines you need a card to get credit for your play.

The DI should keep a low profile, keep low key and stay under the radar. This is another contradiction in thinking. The minute you give that players card in at the crap table, you are going to be tracked forever. So DI's, get used to it. You are a marked player the minute you buy in.

My advice for you is to play your normal game and don't get caught up in the comp craze. If you decide to play their game, do it intelligently. Buy in for $500 and set a stop loss at $300. If you lose $200, you're done. Exit the table. Don't color up. If they ask you to, tell them you're going to another table. The important thing is they have you down as buying in for $500.

Try to establish yourself as a green chip player while the Suit is marking your card. As soon as the Suit walks, regress your bet down to table minimum. Once you set a pattern in that Suit's mind, he may mark your card without checking what you're betting. When you're done playing, ask the Suit to comp your breakfast or buffet. If you have done your homework and built up a rapport with the crew, the comps will come.

Here's one more tip. Stay at a casino that is in a big conglomerate and do most of your playing in those places.

Make sure you check out with a host to get full credit for your play.

22

Top Crap Shooters in the Country

This has got to be the most controversial chapter in the book. When we talk about the best crap shooters in the country, we are talking about instructors and alumni of craps, who not only talk the talk, but walk the walk. These DI's are the best and prove it over and over.

I have played with most of them and some I have watched. One of them I never witnessed in action but his contributions to craps can't be denied. I put him at the top of the list and that's the **Mad Professor**. His knowledge about craps and his willingness to share his knowledge with the world for free is a rare thing in this age. In my book, he is number one.

The **Dice Coach** deserves the number two slot. He is an outstanding instructor. His home is his training camp with a regulation crap table in the family room. He and his wife open the doors of their home for seminars, one on one tune-ups and tournaments. When it comes to craps, the coach is on twenty-four hour call.

Number three goes to *Irish-Setter* for time and energy he spent on managing the Dicesetter.com forum. He also is one of the best instructors I have had the pleasure to play with.

Number four is the Paladin of the dice world. That's *Heavy* (has dice, will travel), He's the seminar king of the dice world. He also is the mastermind of wrong way craps betting and "see a horn, bet a horn" fame.

Soft Touch maybe listed fifth but she rates right up there with the previous four. Not only is she a top shooter, she is a top instructor in positive thinking. She brings energy to the table that is unbelievable. I witnessed three of her long rolls and it was something to behold. She now owns Dicesetter.com.

With all the mystery surrounding the *Mad Professor*, we also have *The Professor* who sits in the sixth spot. He is the master of positive thinking and perception. He can shoot and he can teach.

MV's great website is at www.playing4keeps.com. He also has a dice book out called "Do's and Don'ts of Dice".

Five of these top ranked DI's are shooting instructors and put their money on the line when teaching. Their skills are so evenly matched, that it may not be fair to list them in any certain order. Well it's my book and my opinion, and I listed them for other reasons than just their shooting ability.

Their strong suit is that they all love the game of craps. They all love to teach the game to beginners or experienced players, young or old. If you get the chance, take a lesson from any of them.

23

Crazy Saturday Nights at the Boat

Saturday Night at the Boat or any casino is not favorable to the DI. The DI wants the table all to himself. At the Boat, that will not happen very often. If you are a early morning player and hope to play by yourself, forget it.

Once you buy in at an empty table, the cockroaches appear out of nowhere. Next thing you know, it's you and six chicken feeders at the table. There goes the neighborhood.

Well, Saturday night is much worse but manageable. Saturday night they will have two or three tables in full swing. You can usually find a spot at the table and then maneuver into your favorite spot as the CF's fall by the wayside.

It all started about two and a half years ago after reading **Sharpshooter's** book. With this new-found knowledge, *Lazor* and I took on Trump's boat. After about twenty minutes of jockeying around, we got SR1 and SL1.

I had been practicing for six weeks and this was my maiden voyage as a dice setter.

The dice finally came around and I set for the seven on the come-out and set the hard-way for the point. *Lazor* noted that it was 10 P.M. when I made my first toss. One hour and six minutes later, I sevened-out. *Lazor* said it was one hour five minutes when the dealer corrected him and said it was six minutes. The *Target* got there for half of the run. *Lazor* and the *Target* had back to back mini runs. We decided to color up. *Lazor* was up $1200, I was up $1050 and the *Target* made $500.

The night was still young, so we went next door to the Majestic Star and played for forty-five minutes. We each shot once and made money on all three rolls. We noticed that some of the guys had followed us to the MS.

This good fortune continued for about two months.

It got to the point where my wife would say, are you going to work tonight (Saturday night at the boat).

One of those Saturday nights I was waiting for the rest of the crew to show up and a couple lurkers came over and asked me if we were going to shoot. These same guys seemed to show up at whatever table we played at no matter what time we showed up. Several times I suggested that we play on another night. *Lazor* said, "We always win on Saturday night, why change?"

The hard-way set finally started to turn on me. The more I practiced, the more sevens popped up. I switched over to the V3 and V2 set and things got better. In practice I was putting up big numbers. In the real world I was making small wins and working on my come-out game.

Recently at Trump, *Lazor* and I were at our preferred positions, waiting for the dice to come around, when this tall dude comes up to the table with a fistful of $100 bills. He buys in for a fistful of $100 chips. His only bet is $100 on the eleven. The guy next to him has the dice and throws eleven on the come-out. The dude wins and gives the shooter a $100 chip. Two shooters later another eleven was thrown. Again the dude gives the shooter a black chip. Now he's betting a black chip on eleven on every toss. The next shooter throws two elevens during his short roll. The dude gives him two black chips. I never saw anything like it. The guy is betting eleven on every roll!

Lazor and I are going nuts. We want to get our hands on the dice and throw some elevens before the guy wakes up. Finally I got the dice. Twelve rolls later, no eleven. Same goes for *Lazor*. We were even for the night, but we felt like we lost.

Saturday night at the Empress had its moments. The newest member to our crew, *2Fist* was at SL2. The *Target* was at SR1 and I was at SR2. The *Kooler* was on the hook next to a middle-aged woman who had the dice. None of us were on the pass line. She proceeded to throw five sevens in a row. She was a chicken feeder with a soft throw. Her point was six and she made it in short order. With all the sevens she threw on the come-out, I figured it was time to get on the six and eight. After making the six she threw three more sevens on the come-out. Again we were sleeping and missed out. Now she has five for the point. She threw us a bone by throwing back to back eights and then made her point. Now we all were on the pass line and darn if she didn't throw two more sevens. She caught a ten for the point and sevened-out. She threw eleven sevens in less than twenty tosses. That's a SRR of 1.8.

Where was *Golfer* when we needed him? *Golfer* is the mastermind of the "Hopping Sevens." For those of you who don't know what a "hopping seven" is, check the glossary.

24

Dice Influencer Rules

The Dice Influencer will go over his check list, the minute he walks through the casino door. Is he ready to take on the real life casino? Has he practiced enough to make a difference? Does his skill warrant an SRR of 7.1 or higher? Is his bankroll enough to get started? All these questions and he's not even at the table yet.

The number one rule is **practice**, practice, practice. Number two, **read and learn** every thing you can find on modern craps. Go to a seminar and **take a lesson**. The first time you venture out to test the water, take another DI with you to watch your back. By that I mean have someone along to watch your grip and toss. If you are doing something wrong, you want to catch it before it becomes a habit.

When you arrive at the table, wait till the shooter is done before you put your money and player card down. The crew will appreciate you waiting until the roll is over. They have enough to do at that point, making payouts and placing new bets.

Set your **stop loss** figure. Always know where you stand chip-wise. Make sure you have white chips for **tipping** when you have the dice. Only tip when you have the dice. Tipping when you leave the table won't do you much good when you are gone.

Be nice, be friendly with the crew. If you're grouchy and demanding, they will treat you the same way,

Don't bet on every player. Decide in advance how you are going to play the Chicken Feeders. The hardest part of the game is to stand around waiting for the dice without making a bet. Nobody likes to wait forty-five minutes for the dice to come around and then point seven out. I suppose we could read a book while waiting, but then we are supposed to keep a low profile. Better yet, take a small note book to the table and track all the other shooters. That will keep you busy and out of betting trouble until the dice come your way. It is wise to always make a small bet on the shooter that has the dice just before you. Then it won't be so obvious you're not betting everyone.

Rules are made to be broken and craps players are the biggest offenders.

25

Loose Ends

It doesn't take a brain surgeon to figure out what we are trying accomplish. The casinos know and sometimes I get the feeling that they are laughing up their sleeves at us. I know that I can throw two less sevens then the average Chicken Feeder. The casino bases its odds on the CF or Random Roller. Over a number of sessions, that gives me the advantage. That will give you the advantage too, if you practice what is in this book.

Proposition Bets are not recommended for general consumption. All the bets in the center of the layout have large percentage advantages to the casino. The **Hard-way** bet over time will deplete your bankroll. On one of my better practice sessions, I put the hard-way to the test. I put 72 rolls into the Bone Tracker program using the hard-way set. 71.83% of my tosses were on axis and I only threw 6 hard-ways. The session resulted in a SRR of 6.46. I would have thought that with 52 tosses on axis, I would have produced more hard-ways. Look at the low SRR. My thought is don't set them and don't bet them (hardways).

Muscle Memory is important to your toss. Once you get your arm swing in the groove, repetition will let muscle memory take over. The key is to keep from forming bad habits that your muscle memory could lock in. That's why your grip and delivery is so important.

Books, Seminars and Web Sites are your best bet for answers to your dice setting questions. When it comes down to dice setting, there are **five books** you should read.

You already have read one of them. I recommend you read *Heavy's* latest edition of "Axis Power Craps" and *Sharp Shooter's* book, "Get the Edge at Craps." The fourth book is *Yuri's* "Dice Control for Casino Craps." His chapter on dice sets is a little confusing..

"The Mad Professor's Crap Shooting Bible" will be out soon. This book could set the standard for years to come. I have no doubt that it will be a good seller.

Hardly a month goes by without a **Seminar** on dice control going on someplace. If you want to learn from the best, then I suggest you sign up for one of *Heavy* and *Dice Coaches'* weekend training sessions. Both can be reached at wwwDicecoach.com or www.Axispowercraps.com.

The best **Web Sites** for dice information are the two above and www.Dicesetter.com. The *Mad Professor* is a member of the three Boards and will answer all your crap questions.

Best places to play. My favorite is **Treasure Island**. They have twelve foot tables, friendly table crews, no heat, low bounce factor and decent comps. In the last couple years, it has changed its image to a low key, less children atmosphere.

My first consideration is always the table size. If it is a twelve foot table, I will play. The second consideration is the no-heat factor. Next I consider the friendliness of the table and pit crew. These factors are reasonable in Las Vegas and all the large Mecca areas. At the casino boats, you don't have too many options.

Using these factors, I would put **Bellagio** second. They have a Suit or two that can be over-observant. The same goes for **Mirage** and **Paris**. All three have twelve foot tables with acceptable bounce.

There are two more worth mentioning, even though they don't meet my standard completely. There are casinos that you win at and have a tendency to return to them. The **Barbary Coast** is one of them that has been good to me in the past. My wife loves to play blackjack there, so it is on our must stop list.

The last one I will mention is the **Casino Royale**. It's dark, dirty, and old and only has two tables. It seems to attract the depressed and outer limits crowd. On the plus side, it has $3 tables and 100X odds. Where else in Las Vegas can you eat fast food and shoot craps? After you leave there, you really appreciate where you're staying.

Thirty years ago I played my first game of craps. The scene was at the Desert Inn, 1975. I was with the *Kooler* and *JR*, Back in those days, they called the *Kooler* Mr. B. They were coaching me on how to play the game. *JR* tells me all I have to do is bet the six and eight. So I did. Meanwhile they are making one come bet after another. They had chips all over the box numbers with double odds. Every roll was off and on for them. There I sat with $6 on the six and eight.

After collecting four times I pressed up one unit each and watched the feeding frenzy going on. They were pressing their come bets as fast as they hit. JR tells me to keep pressing the six and eight. I did one more two unit press and sat back and collected that green chip and three whites every time they hit. When the smoke cleared I was over a hundred dollars ahead. My two shipwrecked friends had more money on the table when the seven came, than they had in the rack.

The moral of this experience is that the advice they gave me, thirty years ago, is still good today. Play those six and eights and use a regression strategy based on your SRR. Make some quick hits and get your money off the board.

The old adage of playing the pass line and making two or three come bets is disappearing fast. I rarely see any come bettors anymore. I guess they learned their lesson. It takes two comes to dance and only one place to score.

While working on this book, my daughter and her husband came over for a visit. They saw I was working on the book and my daughter asked if she could ask me a question. I said go ahead. She says, "Dad, I read your second book and when we were in Las Vegas, we did everything you said to do. While playing with you we noticed you were doing everything different. What gives?" I told her that book was outdated and we were entering the modern age of craps. Dice setting is the new game in town. That's the reason for this book.

Dice Control is a misconception in wordage. We will never be able to say we have total control over the dice. With the rubber baby bumper pyramids for a back wall and the speed bumps under the layout, total control is close to impossible. We can control the takeoff and where they land, but after that it's a crap shoot.

All we can do is try to be as consistent as possible with our set, grip and toss. We must play to our **SRR** to bring the casino down to our level. Instead of referring to our skills as controlling the dice, we should refer to them as influencing them.

Using the right dice set and keeping the dice on axis is all we can do to gain a favorable result. Once we get past the come-out, every throw is a winner as long as it's not a seven. You may not always win chips but you will still have the dice for another roll.

Is the **Revolution** here to stay? Yes and no. Yes, dice setting and influencing is the wave of the future. As to the participants, that's a gray area. The leaders of the movement are still sensitive about past differences. When I checked the Internet this morning, I discovered this post from *the Lion* discussing the *"Mad Professors Craps Shooting Bible:"* **MP,**

"And what if **FS** and **JP** incorporate all your stuff into their barnstorming classes, causing incredible DI countermeasures by casinos? Will you still be able to play as often as you are now?"

MP's answer to *the Lion*: "I anticipate that I will still be profitably shooting craps long after those two sorry-assed warbirds that you mentioned find their broken-down carcasses mothballed at Davis-Monthan AMARC."

For those of you that don't know, **FS** is the self proclaimed best gaming author in the world. A self-titled expert at all table games. He also claims to have had rolls of 100-150 tosses. When it comes to craps, he is a great writer of fiction.

As far as loose ends go, this is about as loose as it gets. When you talk about fictional characters, **FS** takes the cake. He has been touting the **"Captain"** for more years than I care to remember. No one has seen this fictional character. Yet, he is given credit as being the first rhythm roller to set the dice. With the vast amounts of money he has been reported as winning, according to **Pope Frank**, you would have thought someone would have spotted him.

The **Mad Professor's** book will have his invisible character too. That would be himself. At least you can read his writing on the wall.

For the sake of this book, I would like to introduce my invisible character, Mr. **Craps.** He plays in the Chicago area and stays below the radar. **Mr. Craps** has a beautiful toss. He hits and runs. I think the **Golfer** spotted him one time.

26

Wrapping It All Up

We have covered the things you need to know and practice to become a **Dice Influencer**. Now it's up to you. I can show you how to do it, but in reality you will have to do it for yourself. If you need a lesson before you develop bad habits, contact any of us on the web sites mentioned in this book.

Dice control starts with your **selection of a table** and **position** at the table. Try to get your best position at the table. In time you can branch out and train yourself to play from other positions.

Learn how to **set the dice** so that it becomes second nature to you. Practice using all the sets for the first two or three weeks. This will help you become more familiar with the different combinations. You can use any one for the come-out. Pick out a set with less sevens probability. That would be the **V2, V3 and X6's**. For practicing your on-axis toss, use the hard-way set, so you can see the results.

The **Grip** should be comfortable and easy to make the **pickup**. Try all the grips. Physical problems with your hand will more than likely determine what grip to use. When you pick up the dice you should be facing the dealer. The dice should be facing you. **Finger pressure** on the dice should be minimal. Some say that the least amount of skin you have on the dice the better off you are. By moving your fingers up or down the seam of the dice, you can control the spin on the dice. Again it's a matter of choice based on your finger strength.

Delivering the dice should be done in a manner so that the dice go no higher than your shoulder. This is also a personal option. If you are tossing from the deck, the angle of take off is between **thirty and forty-five degrees**. This will vary on different tables depending on the bounce. To control the bounce, you will need a **low, slow and soft delivery.**

Keeping Records will help you determine if your **SRR** is progressing. It also will help you determine what your **signature number** is. Your signature number will play an important part in your betting strategy.

Acquire a **practice table**. You can make one, buy one or use the dining room table. You will find that all the tables in your home are approximately twenty-nine inches off the floor. Most casino tables are twenty-eight to twenty-nine inches from the floor. Do your tossing from eight feet.

Money Management and Betting Strategy goes hand in hand. Get some chips and a felt layout and try different strategies. Work on the regression, pressing and the Iron Cross strategy. Use your **SRR** to tell how long you should stay on board. Setting a **stop-loss** figure will save you money in the long run.

When you think you are ready for **DI** play in a real live casino, take time to review this book. When you get there don't bet on every shooter. The "five count" is not for the DI. A good DI will hit and run. The bets he does make will come in early and he will pull them down inside his SRR ratio. When the DI stays in the game longer than his SRR ratio, it is because he has regressed his bets so that he no longer has money in jeopardy. If the run continues, he will press his bets on winning numbers, returning at least fifty percent to his chip rack.

Don't forget to **tip** when you have the dice. A single white chip on the pass line will do until you get some winners. If you're hitting numbers, you can throw a white chip on the odds.

Be cool, be humble, be low key and be nice. The dealers will respect you and may be helpful later on. Keep an eye open for undue **heat** from the suits or box-man. It may not concern you but you want to be aware of what they're watching. I very rarely miss the back wall, but when I do, it usually is ignored by the crew and suits. If you do get heat for setting the dice, consider leaving immediately.

There you have it. The technical stuff and basic crap has been eliminated. If you are an average player losing more than winning, then you're ready for this book. I've kept it plain, simple and to the point. I included some of my experiences so you can see what can be accomplished. What's in this book can change your dice playing life.

Good luck and good shooting. Practice, practice and practice some more. That's a wrap.

GLOSSARY

✦

Terms and Handles Used in this Book
and Outside

ACTION—The bets you make or the fights you get into with other players.

ANY CRAPS—A one roll bet looking for a 2, 3, or 12; and the guff you take from the pit critters.

ANY SEVEN—A one roll bet looking for a seven that is not hopping.

BAR 12—Disadvantage to the Don't Pass and Don't Come better. A 12 neither wins nor loses.

BETTING LIMIT—Maximum bet accepted on any number—Amount of money in your pocket..

BOXMAN—The lazy guy in the suit, seated at the center of the table, who watches everything that transpires in a craps game.

BUY-IN—The amount of chips you acquire when arriving at the table. Your donation to the casino building fund.

BUY THE FOUR OR TEN—Paying a 5% commission to the casino in order to be paid the correct odds of 2-1 on placing the four or ten.

C & E, CRAPS-ELEVEN—A bet that craps (2, 3, or 12) or eleven shows on the next roll of the dice.

CHICKEN FEEDER—A random roller who throws the dice like he's feeding chickens.

CHIPS—Tokens issued by the casino in place of money, having the equivalent of cash.

COLOR-UP—Having your chips of small denomination changed to chips of higher denomination so you won't have so many to carry to the cashier's cage. It's an excuse to record your winnings or losses.

COME BET—After the come-out roll, it is a bet that the dice will repeat a number.

COME BOX—Area on the table layout where a Come bet is made.

COME-OUT ROLL—First roll of the dice before a number is established.

COMPS—Receiving complimentary meals, rooms, points or service; which are given to players in exchange for their action.

CRAPS—When a 2, 3, or 12 shows on board and the player gives a response.

DEAD-CAT—Master of the dead-cat bounce.

DEALER—Person who handles your bets and pays you when you win. He will answer all your silly questions.

DI—Dice Influencer—One who tries to change the outcome of probability.

DICE—A pair of cubes with numbers indicated by dots called pips, which are rolled to determine payoffs and losses. The numbers on the opposite sides of the dice always total seven

DICE COACH—Premier instructor and top shooter in the Las Vegas area.

DICEKETEERS—Lazor, The Target and 009.

DICE SETTER—A shooter who meticulously sets the dice a certain way before each roll.

DOEY-DON'T BETTER—A person who bets on the Pass, Come, Don't Pass and Don't Come at the same time.

DON'T COME BET—A bet made after the come-out roll, that the shooter will not make his point.

DOMINATOR—TV star and Premier player from the GTC camp.

DON'T PASS BET—A bet made on the come-out roll, that the shooter will not make his point.

DOUBLE ODDS BET—A free odds bet, made at double the amount of the original bet.

EASY WAY—The opposite of hard-way. Rolling a 4, 6, 8, or 10 where no pairs show.

EVEN MONEY—Being paid at 1-1. Bet one chip, get paid one chip.

FIELD BETS—A bet that the next roll of the dice will come up 2, 3, 4, 9, 10, 11, or 12.

FIRE BET—Betting that you can make all the point numbers 4, 5, 6, 8, 9 and 10 before you seven-out.

2-FIST—One of the up and coming players in the Chicago area.

FIVE COUNT—After a point is established, a count of five rolls is waited on, before placing any more bets.

FLOORMAN—The person that approves your credit, rates you and returns your player card to you and wishes you good luck. If he likes you he will call you by your initial, such as; "good luck Mr. B."

FS—Writes gaming fiction.

GOLFER—Premier Midwest player and mastermind of the "Hopping sevens" play.

HEAVY—Premier Instructor, Crap Fest coordinator and top shooter in the Southwest.

HARDWAYS—A wager that the dice will come up 2-2, 3-3, 4-4 or 5-5 before the seven comes up, or before it's made the "easy" way.

HIGH ROLLER—A bettor who wagers large sums of money at the craps table.

HIT—A number rolled, that pays off.

HOPPING SEVENS—A bet that seven will come on the next roll; in a specific way (as 4/3).

HORN BET—A one-roll wager on the 2. 3, 11, and 12.

HOT ROLL—Dice that are continually passing and held by the same shooter for a long period of time before the seven-out.

HOTSHOOTER—Premier West Coast player.

INSIDE NUMBERS—Numbers 5, 6, 8, and 9.

IRISHSETTER—Creator of the best Craps Website on the Internet, Premier instructor and shooter.

JP—Sells gaming systems.

LAZOR—Midwest player with tons of potential.

MAD DOG—Creator of the Bone Tracker program. Top player and instructor.

MAD PROFESSOR—Could be the best dice mind in North America. Watch for his book.

MARTINI4NATE—Loud shirt fashion plate of the dice world.

LAYOUT—Imprint on a felt surface covering the crap table where wagers are placed.

ODDS—The correct ratio determining whether or not an event will occur at a crap table.

OFF—A call, by a player, that his bet will not be working on the next roll of the dice.

ON—Bets working.

ON-AXIS TOSS—Toss that rotates with backspin on both dice and remains together till landing side-by-side.

OUTSIDE NUMBERS—The number 4, 5, 9 and 10.

PASS—A winning decision where a shooter makes a point.

PASS LINE—The area on the table layout where a Pass Line wager is made.

PAYOFF—To be paid on a winning wager.

PIT BOSS—Supervises all crap tables in an area called the pit. He handles anything that the floor manager can't.

PIT CREATURES-They are the guys in dark suits, standing behind the crap tables and drinking coffee.

PLACE NUMBERS, PLACE BETS—A wager on the numbers 4, 5, 6, 8, 9 or 10 made in the place box on the layout.

PLAYER—Gambler or bettor who puts money where his mouth is.

PLAYER CARD—Plastic card that looks like a credit card, that is turned in to the Floor Manager at the table games for tracking purposes, for comps.

POINT—The number 4, 5, 6, 8, 9 or 10, when rolled on the come-out roll.

PRESS—To increase a bet by one unit or doubling the bet.

PROPOSITION BETS—All bets in the middle of the table.

RAIL OR RACK—Grooved area at the crap table where you place your chips not being bet.

RHYTHM ROLLER—A shooter who rolls the same way, time after time.

RIGHT BETTOR—One who bets with the dice.

RR—Random Roller is a person who throws the dice any old way.

ROLL—A single roll of the dice or a series of throws, until the shooter sevens-out.

SEVEN-OUT—Throwing a seven after a point has been established, ending the roll.

SHARPSHOOTER—Came out with one of the first books on Dice control

SHOOTER—Player who rolls or throws the dice.

SOFT TOUCH—She rates with the best shooters out there. Great inspirational instructor and group coordinator.

SR—Stick Right—The first shooting position to the right of the stick person facing the box-man.

SL—Stick Left—First shooting position to the left of stick person facing the box-man.

SUITS—The pit critters with dark suits and bored looks on their faces.

STICKMAN—He calls the game and uses the stick to move the dice to the shooter.

TABLE MINIMUM—The least amount of money that you can bet at the table.

THE KOOLER—He's my lawyer and proof reader.

THE LION—He is the hardest working student of the game when he's not chasing women or making movies.

THE PROFESSOR—Great instructor on Dice, positive thinking and inspirational thought.

THE TARGET—Out of the GTC school and plays craps eight days a week.

TIP or TOKE—A gratuity or bribe given to a dealer to leave us alone when we are shooting..

UNIT—The basic amount wagered on the Pass Line, Come or Place area.

WORKING—Bets that are in place and can win or lose on the next roll of the dice.

WRONG BETTOR—One who bets against the dice.

CHARLIE009—PHD—Doctoral of Dice Influencing.

Books by the Author

ISBN: 1-59129-478-9
www.publishamerica.com

ISBN: 1-58898-194-0
www.greatunpublished.com

This book is directed at the beginner with little or no knowledge of the game.

This book is for the average player who knows the game and needs a eye opening review.

978-0-595-39083-0
0-595-39083-8

Printed in the United States
107920LV00002B/4/A

9 780595 390830